Loyalty
By Aaron Fields

Copyright © 2021 Aaron Fields. All rights reserved.

Published by The Write Perspective, LLC

Dallas, Texas,

All rights reserved. No part of this book shall be reproduced or transmitted in any form or by any means, electronic, mechanical, magnetic, photographic including photocopying, recording or by any information storage and retrieval system, without prior written permission of the publisher. No copyright liability is assumed with respect to the use of the information contained in this book. Even though every precaution has taken in preparation of this book, the publisher/author assumes no responsibility for errors or omissions. Neither is any liability assumed for any damage that results from the use of the information in this book.

ISBN: 978-1-953962-50-8

If you are born with the gift of loyalty, you must be very careful who you apply that to.

Aaron Fields

If you're born with the gift of loyalty, be careful who you apply that to. Most people are not loyal, they will turn on you.

Loyalty is a gift, but it's also a curse.

If you're loyal to the wrong person, life will get worse.

It takes time to know the person and what their motives are.

People are very sneaky, they'll creep up like a jaguar.

Believe me, people will come into your life for a season.

When people walk out of your life, it's for a reason.

Be careful who you bring into your life, always stay alert.

If you're not careful, you'll end up getting hurt.

Most people say they're loyal, but is that true?

If life gets hard, will they quit on you?

Loyalty is about being genuine, and having someone's best interest at heart. If the relationship is mutual, you'll never depart.

Loyalty is not earned through words, but with action.

Don't allow yourself to get hurt, otherwise it'll be a chain reaction.

Food For Thought

It's important to understand that most people in this world are not loyal and they don't have true integrity.

If a person's word means nothing to them, then it should mean nothing to you.

Be careful when certain people try to initiate a relationship with you.

Be careful who you align yourself with.

Use proper discernment and discretion when dealing with others.

Don't let your gift of loyalty be your curse.

www.ingramcontent.com/pod-product-compliance
Lightning Source LLC
Chambersburg PA
CBHW041527090426
42736CB00035B/40